For Grandma Mueller, a maker of magic.
—B. H.

To Lydia, Chloe, Madelyn, Moses, and Naomi—
may you all discover your passions and follow your dreams.
—K. C.

Text copyright © 2020 Brooke Hartman
Illustrations copyright © 2020 Kathryn Carr

First published in 2020 by Page Street Kids
an imprint of
Page Street Publishing Co.
27 Congress Street, Suite 105
Salem, MA 01970
www.pagestreetpublishing.com

Distributed by Macmillan, sales in Canada by The Canadian Manda Group

20 21 22 23 24 CCO 5 4 3 2 1

ISBN-13: 978-1-62414-941-2
ISBN-10: 1-62414-941-3

CIP data for this book is available from the Library of Congress.

This book was typeset in Dragon Serial.
The illustrations were created with hand-cut paper, photography, and digital tools.

Printed and bound in Shenzhen, Guangdong, China

Page Street Publishing uses only materials from suppliers who are
committed to responsible and sustainable forest management.

Page Street Publishing protects our planet by donating to nonprofits like
The Trustees, which focuses on local land conservation.

trustees

Lotte's Magical Paper Puppets

The Woman Behind the First Animated Feature Film

Brooke Hartman

illustrated by Kathryn Carr

PAGE STREET KIDS

Long before a cartoon mouse,
Or Snow White found a little house,
There was a girl named Charlotte.
Everyone called her Lotte.

Lotte loved the cinema:
The way the actors danced and swayed,
Music's playful serenade,
Lights that *wink-wink-winked.*

Everyone clapped and smiled.
The cinema was magic.

Lotte wanted to make her own magic.

So she gathered up some things:
A stack of cards, some wiry string,
Scissors that *snip-snip-snipped*.

Then Lotte made some puppets:
Cinderella, always sweeping.
A beauty in a castle, sleeping.
Two loves torn apart,
A lovestruck heart,
And a star
So bright.

But for magic, Lotte needed the cinema.
For the cinema, she needed film.

And she needed more puppets:
A clockwork pony flying, leaping.
A trove of treasure for the reaping.
A princess true.
The good witch who
Saves the prince,
Achmed.

Then Lotte found a lamp of brass,
A table and a pane of glass,
A camera that *click-click-clicked.*

But she still needed film.

Her good friends said, "We understand.
We have dreams, too. We'll lend a hand,"
And gave her lots of film.

Rolls, and rolls, and rolls
Of film.

At last, Lotte was ready for the cinema.
Ready for magic!

Her paper puppets danced and swayed.
Music played a serenade.
Lights *wink-wink-winked.*

Everyone clapped and smiled—

Almost everyone.

A man rose up in Lotte's land.
With twisted words, he clenched his hand
And made demands
That he command
All magic.

His words made many people scared.
Soon, sounds of fighting filled the air
With sirens blaring,
Fires flaring,
Guns that *tat-tat-tatted*.

Lotte was afraid, too.

So she gathered up her things:
Her lamp and glass, her wiry string,
Her camera and scissors.

And she ran
From hateful words and poisoned air,
Desperate for a new land where
No sirens blared,
No fires flared,
And her magic
Was safe.

For many years, Lotte roamed,
Searching for another home.

All the while, she made more puppets:
A young boy up a chimney creeping.
A true heart stolen for the keeping.
A cat in boots,
A magic flute,
And the hero,
Papageno.

Then one day, Lotte had to go back.
To help her mother, dearly missed.
Back to the land with the men
And their fists.

They ordered Lotte to make new puppets.
Puppets made to fright and scare,
With hands that clench and eyes that glare
And drums that *brum-brum-brum*.

But Lotte was done being afraid.
She feared no fist, no gun, no hand.
Her magic lived by no command.

So instead, she made:
A lovely princess, always weeping.
A young man to her castle, leaping.
A goose made of gold,
A sight to behold,
To make the princess
Laugh.

She hung her puppets up to share,
In window panes, in shops, up stairs,
while everywhere
Through smoky air
Bombs *boom-boom-boomed.*

Her puppets made the people smile.
Made them remember song and rhyme
And days from once upon a time.

Until at last there rose a cheer:
"The war is done!" No one could hear
Sirens blaring,
Fires flaring,
Guns that *tat-tat-tatted*.

So once again, with joyful heart,
Lotte gathered up her art
And set her magic
Free.

In cinemas both near and far,
The people watched in wondrous awe
As Lotte's puppets danced and swayed,
Music played a serenade,
A brother left a trail of crumbs,
A girl was born, small as a thumb,
A beanstalk rose into the sky,
Aladdin found his princess bride,
And lights *wink-wink-winked*
Like stars.

Through war, through time, her art lives on
For all the world, for everyone,
So you can clap
And you can smile

For Lotte and her magic.

❦ Author's Note ❧

Even if you hadn't heard of Lotte Reiniger before this story, you've likely seen animated films influenced by her work, from the end credits of Lemony Snicket's *A Series of Unfortunate Events* to the "Tale of the Three Brothers" in *Harry Potter and the Deathly Hallows*. Born in Germany in 1899, Lotte was enamored with shadow puppets and the cinema from a young age. She combined these arts to create innovative films—including the first feature length animated film, *The Adventures of Prince Achmed*, over a decade before Walt Disney's *Snow White!*

With a lamp, a table, and panes of glass, Lotte invented a multiplane camera to make stop motion animation with her paper puppets. Multiplane cameras work by layering sheets of glass to place artwork on, which helps create depth and motion. Unlike a puppet show, you can't see anyone moving the puppets in Lotte's films because their positions were changed between each photograph. Each of her films took years to complete, as each second of the movie required twenty-four separate photos.

Over her lifetime, Lotte made over eighty silhouette puppet films, many of which are based on timeless fairy tales. Even when she returned to Germany during World War II to care for her ailing mother, Lotte refused to bend to the Nazis' strict propaganda film regulations, and instead created another fairy tale film: *The Golden Goose*. Her whimsical animated films taught a war-torn world that light can overcome darkness, and humanity is nothing without the magic of hope.

❦ Artist's Note ❧

It was important to me to honor Lotte's fine craftsman-ship by replicating the techniques that went into making her art. Using a variety of papers and a small pair of scissors, she would cut out intricate and expressive silhouettes and twist tiny pieces of wire by hand to connect the parts. These puppets were then filmed using her multiplane camera.

For the illustrations in this book, I have created my versions of Lotte's puppets and intertwined them with my own whimsical style of paper cutting. My art is influenced by the storybooks from my childhood and a German type of folk art called *scherenschnitte* (pronounced share-in-shnit-ta) which translates literally to "scissor cuts."

❦ Some of Lotte Reiniger's Famous Silhouette Films ❦

Sleeping Beauty 1922

The Adventures of Prince Achmed 1926

Papageno 1935

Aladdin and the Magic Lamp 1954

Hansel and Gretel 1955

Aucassin and Nicolette 1975

The Four Seasons 1980

1922 Cinderella

1935 Puss in Boots

1944 The Golden Goose

1954 Thumbelina

1956 Jack and the Beanstalk

1976 The Rose and the Ring

"I believe more in the truth of fairy tales than that found in the newspapers."
—Lotte Reiniger

❦ Bibliography ❦

Feaster, Felicia. *The Adventures of Prince Achmed.* Turner Classic Movies. http://www.tcm.com/this-month/article/28082%7C0/The-Adventures-of-Prince-Achmed.html.

Grace, Whitney. *Lotte Reiniger, Pioneer of Film Animation.* Jefferson, North Carolina: MacFarland & Company, Inc., 2017.

Isaacs, John, dir. *The Art of Lotte Reiniger.* 1970; London, U.K.: Primrose Productions.

"Lotte Reiniger." The Internet Movie Database. http://www.imdb.com/lottereiniger.

Reiniger, Lotte. *Shadow Puppets, Shadow Theatres, and Shadow Films.* Reprint Edition, Boston: Plays, Inc. 1975.